THE TIGER TOTEM
SHAMANIC PRACTICES AND
SPIRITUAL MEDICINE

Valerio Barsacchi

THE TIGER TOTEM

To all the totem animals, always present by our side, silent and wise guardians guiding us on our path. Especially to my beloved wolf, symbol of strength, loyalty, and wisdom. May you continue to inspire and protect all those who seek your guidance. With infinite gratitude, I dedicate this book to you and to all the totems that accompany humanity with love and wisdom.

Valerio Barsacchi

THE TIGER TOTEM

CONTENS

In the silence of the night and the heart of the forest,
the totems whisper ancient wisdom.
Guardians of dreams, silent guides,
they lead us with light steps.
With eyes of fire and wings of wind,
they bring strength and light to our path.
Wild souls, loyal spirits,
always by our side,
in eternal enchantment.

INTRODUCTION

Welcome to this journey of discovery into the world of animal totems, a fascinating universe rich in ancestral wisdom that deeply connects us to nature and our inner self. Animal totems are not mere symbols; they are spiritual guides, protectors, and teachers who accompany us along the path of life, offering precious insights and inner strength.

This book was born from the desire to share the beauty and power of animal totems, with a particular focus on the tiger, a totem that embodies qualities such as strength, courage, and determination. Through these pages, we will explore the world of animal totems, discovering how we can encounter and connect with our totem, and how we can integrate their teachings into our daily lives.

We will begin with an overview of animal totems, explaining what they are and why they are important. We will learn techniques for discovering our totem through shamanic journeys and other introspective methods. We will explore how to recognize the signs and synchronicities that indicate attraction towards a specific totem and how to interpret dreams and visions involving these powerful symbols.

In the second part of the book, we will focus on the tiger, examining in detail its shamanic significance, the characteristics of people who have the tiger as their totem, and how we can invoke and work with the tiger's energy in our daily lives. We will also discover the associations and correspondences of the tiger with numbers, stones, planets, and deities, and provide practical exercises for building a dedicated altar, creating amulets and talismans, and practicing meditations and rituals guided by the tiger.

This book is designed to be a comprehensive and accessible guide, suitable for both newcomers to this world and those with some experience. The goal is to provide practical tools and inspiration to help you connect deeply with animal totems and integrate their wisdom into your daily life.

Prepare your spirit for a fascinating journey, letting yourself be guided by animal totems through the forests of your inner self.

WHAT ARE ANIMAL TOTEMS?

Animal totems are powerful and sacred symbols that have accompanied humanity through centuries of history and diverse cultures. The concept of an animal totem varies slightly from one tradition to another, but the essence remains the same: they represent a deep connection between humans and the animal kingdom, serving as spiritual guides and protectors. Among Indigenous peoples, such as Native Americans, animal totems are considered guardian spirits that accompany a person throughout life, offering wisdom, strength, and protection.

In many cultures, animal totems are not chosen by the individual but are revealed through dreams, visions, or shamanic rituals. These animals are seen as embodiments of specific qualities and can represent character traits, innate abilities, or spiritual lessons that the person needs to learn. Each animal totem has unique attributes and brings with it a set of teachings that help the individual overcome life's challenges.

The role of animal totems as spiritual guides and protectors is central to their definition. They serve as intermediaries between the physical and spiritual worlds, offering a direct link to the wisdom of nature. Animal totems are often invoked during ceremonies and rituals to ask for guidance, strength, or healing. Their symbolic presence in sacred objects, tattoos, or amulets serves as a constant reminder to the individual of their protection and the teachings they offer.

The connection with an animal totem can be experienced

in various ways: through observing the animal's behavior, meditation, dreams, or everyday life experiences. This unique and personal relationship strengthens the sense of belonging and balance with the natural world, encouraging a more conscious and harmonious life.

The Importance of Totems in Daily Life

Animal totems have a profound and pervasive influence on the daily lives of those who recognize and honor them. They are not just spiritual symbols but represent qualities and abilities that can be practically applied in everyday life. Their presence can inspire positive changes, provide guidance in difficult decisions, and offer a sense of protection and comfort.

For example, a person whose totem is the wolf might draw inspiration from the wolf's loyalty and cooperation. In a work environment, this could translate into a greater inclination to work as part of a team, valuing each member's contribution and building an atmosphere of trust and collaboration. In personal relationships, the wolf teaches the importance of loyalty and mutual support, helping to build strong and lasting bonds.

Another example could be the eagle totem, which embodies vision and freedom. Those with the eagle as their totem may be guided to develop a clear vision of their goals and pursue them with determination, without being limited by immediate circumstances. The eagle also teaches how to look at situations from a higher perspective, assessing challenges with wisdom and finding innovative solutions.

Animal totems can also influence how we face personal challenges and difficulties. Drawing inspiration from the resilience of the bear, the patience of the turtle, or the agility of the cat can provide useful strategies for overcoming obstacles. These animals remind us that we possess the necessary qualities within ourselves to face life with strength and grace.

In addition to directly influencing behavior and decisions, animal totems can also serve as symbols of introspection and personal growth. Reflecting on the characteristics of one's totem can lead to greater self-awareness and a path of self-improvement. For example, understanding the curious and playful nature of the otter may encourage a person to rediscover joy and creativity in their life.

In conclusion, animal totems not only enrich the spiritual dimension of our existence but also offer practical tools and inspiration to enhance our daily lives. Through their wisdom, we can learn to live more consciously, harmoniously, and authentically, recognizing and developing the qualities that help us realize our full potential.

HOW TO DISCOVER YOUR ANIMAL TOTEM

Introduction to the Shamanic Journey

The shamanic journey is an ancient and powerful spiritual practice, used by many indigenous cultures to connect with the spirit world and obtain guidance and wisdom. This method allows you to meet your animal totem, discovering the guide animal that accompanies and protects you along the path of life.

The shamanic journey is based on the belief that there are spiritual worlds parallel to ours, accessible through altered states of consciousness. These worlds are populated by spirit guides, animal totems, and other spiritual entities that offer teachings and support. Shamans, or spiritual healers, use the shamanic journey to explore these worlds, receive visions, and bring back knowledge useful to the community.

The origins and significance of the shamanic journey are found in the indigenous traditions of the world, from Native Americans to Siberian peoples, from Australian Aborigines to the peoples of Africa. In all these cultures, the shamanic journey is seen as a sacred and respected practice, requiring preparation and pure intention. It is considered a means to connect with ancestral wisdom, heal the soul, and find one's place in the world.

To meet your animal totem, the shamanic journey proves to be an extremely effective tool. During the journey, you enter a state of light trance or deep meditation, which allows access to a higher level of consciousness. In this state, it is possible to meet your animal totem, receive messages and teachings, and establish a lasting connection with it. The shamanic journey is usually performed using the sound of a drum or other rhythmic instruments, such as rattles. These instruments help to achieve a shamanic trance in a simple, natural, safe, and stress-free way for the physical body. For the experience, you can also use drumming or rattling tracks, readily available online or in the form of recordings.

Preparation for the Shamanic Journey

To prepare for the shamanic journey, it is helpful to practice meditations and breathing techniques that aid in relaxing the mind and body. A simple breathing exercise can make a big difference. Start by finding a comfortable position in a quiet place. Sit comfortably, with your back straight and your feet firmly on the ground. Inhale slowly through your nose, counting to four. Hold your breath for a couple of seconds, then exhale slowly through your mouth, counting to six. Repeat this breathing cycle for a few minutes until you feel your body relax and your mind calm down.

As you breathe deeply, imagine a golden light entering your body with each inhale. This light purifies and relaxes every part of you, dissolving tensions and negative thoughts. With each exhale, let go of everything that weighs you down and worries you. Continue breathing this way until you feel completely relaxed and centered.

Establishing a ritual before the shamanic journey can help you enter the right mindset. You can light a candle, burn incense, or say a prayer, creating a sacred and serene environment. Ensure that you won't be disturbed during the journey. Turn off your phone and inform others that you will be unavailable for a while. This will allow you to focus entirely on the experience without interruptions.

Approach the journey with an open mind and no specific expectations. Each experience is unique and meaningful in its own way, and maintaining an open and receptive attitude will help you get the most out of your shamanic journey.

Practical Guide to the Shamanic Journey

Before embarking on a shamanic journey, it is essential to adequately prepare the environment, the tools, and your mindset. Choose a quiet and safe place where you won't be disturbed. This space should be clean and orderly, possibly decorated with sacred or natural objects that help create a spiritual atmosphere.

The tools traditionally used for the shamanic journey include drums, rattles, incense, and candles. The drum, in particular, is considered a means to connect with the heartbeat of the Earth and facilitate passage to the spiritual worlds. If you don't have a drum, you can use a recording of rhythmic beats to help you enter a meditative state. These rhythmic sounds help to reach a shamanic trance naturally and safely, facilitating access to an altered state of consciousness without stress on the physical body.

The mindset with which you approach the shamanic

journey is equally important. It is crucial to enter this state with respect, humility, and a clear intention. Take time to reflect on your intention before beginning, asking for guidance and protection for your journey.

Detailed Steps on How to Conduct a Shamanic Journey

As previously discussed, start your shamanic journey by finding a quiet place where you can sit or lie down comfortably. To create a sacred atmosphere, light a candle or incense. This will help purify the environment and prepare your mind for the experience you are about to undertake. Take a few deep breaths, allowing your body and mind to relax completely.

When you feel ready, begin the journey. If you are using a drum, start beating a steady, hypnotic rhythm. Alternatively, you can use a drumming recording. Close your eyes and focus your attention on the rhythm, letting the sound guide you into a light trance state.

Imagine yourself in a natural place that is familiar and comfortable to you, such as a forest, beach, or mountain. Look for a natural passage, such as a cave, a hollow between tree roots, or an opening between rocks, which can lead you to the lower world. If you can't find a natural passage, you can create one with your imagination. The goal is to enter a tunnel that goes downward. Follow this tunnel to the end, even if you experience a sensation of falling into the void. This experience is normal and part of the process of accessing the spirit world.

Once you reach the end of the tunnel, you will find yourself in another world, the spirit world. From here, you can begin to explore and seek your totem. Imagine walking along a path in this new environment. You might encounter various animals along the way. When you meet an animal that seems particularly significant, stop and observe it carefully. Ask the animal if it is your totem. Pay attention to how it responds: it might communicate with you through words, images, or sensations. If the animal confirms that it is your totem, ask what teachings it has for you. Listen carefully to the messages you receive, which may come in the form of advice, symbolic images, or feelings.

When you feel the journey is complete, thank your animal totem for its guidance. Retrace your steps back to the starting point of the tunnel. Ascend the tunnel, and once outside, slowly bring your attention back to your physical body and open your eyes.

During the shamanic journey, it is common to experience vivid visions, intense emotions, and a deep sense of connection. Don't worry if your initial experiences aren't very clear or if you don't immediately encounter your animal totem. Practice and patience are essential. The experiences can be interpreted as symbols or messages from your subconscious and the spiritual world. Even if you encounter an animal that is not your totem, it may still have an important message for you. Keep a journal of your experiences to reflect on them and find deeper meanings over time.

Through these preparation exercises and the practical guide to the shamanic journey, you can begin to explore the world of animal totems and discover your spirit animal if you don't already know it.

ATTRACTION TO A SPECIFIC TOTEM

An animal totem can manifest in our lives in mysterious and meaningful ways, often through signs and synchronicities that capture our attention. Recognizing these signs requires an open and attentive mind, as a totem can present itself in many different forms. You might notice that a particular animal appears repeatedly in your dreams, in conversations, in the media you consume, or even during your daily walks. These repeated encounters are not mere coincidences but rather indications that this animal is trying to communicate with you.

Synchronicity is one of the primary tools through which animal totems make themselves known. You might, for example, start seeing images of a certain animal everywhere, hearing stories about this animal from different people, or even encountering it in nature. Whenever you notice these signs, it is important to take note and reflect on the circumstances and emotions you are experiencing at that moment. These details can offer valuable clues about why the animal totem is trying to enter your life and what message it has for you.

Dreams are another powerful means of communication between us and animal totems. In dreams, our mind is free from the constraints of daily reality, allowing our subconscious to reveal important messages. Animals that appear in dreams often represent qualities or lessons that our animal totem wants to convey to us. To remember and interpret dreams related to animal totems, it is helpful to keep a dream journal next to your bed. As

13

soon as you wake up, immediately write down everything you remember about the dream, including details about the animals present, their actions, and the emotions you experienced.

When interpreting dreams, consider both the traditional symbolism of the animals and the personal context of the dream. For example, dreaming of a wolf might symbolize protection and community, but if you feel frightened by the wolf in the dream, it could indicate that you have fears or anxieties related to your connection with this totem. Reflecting on these aspects will help you better understand the message of the dream.

There are specific techniques to delve deeper into dream interpretation. An effective practice is reflective meditation on dreams, where, in a state of relaxation, you mentally revisit the dream and focus on the details that stood out to you. Ask your animal totem to reveal further meanings or to show you how to apply the dream's messages in your daily life.

It is not uncommon for dreams and visions to be unclear at first. Their interpretation may take time and introspection. Maintain an attitude of openness and trust in the process, knowing that every dream and vision contributes to your connection with the animal totem and your spiritual growth. Through attention to signs and synchronicities and the interpretation of dreams and visions, you can discover which animal totem is attracted to you and what it has to teach you. These methods will help you build a deeper and more meaningful relationship with them.

BENEFITS OF CONNECTING WITH ANIMAL TOTEMS

Connecting with animal totems offers a wide range of benefits that can significantly enhance our daily lives. These benefits are not limited to those who recognize a particular animal as their main totem but are accessible to anyone willing to open themselves to the wisdom and qualities that each totem represents.

Applying Totem Qualities in Daily Life

The characteristics and powers of animal totems can be utilized to improve various aspects of our lives. Each totem brings with it a set of unique qualities that can be integrated into our daily routine to help us become better versions of ourselves.

For example, the wolf is known for its loyalty and ability to work in groups. Applying these qualities in the workplace means valuing the contribution of each team member and creating an environment of trust and collaboration. In personal relationships, the loyalty of the wolf reminds us of the importance of being present and supporting our loved ones, building strong and lasting bonds.

The eagle, with its sharp vision and free spirit, teaches us to maintain a clear perspective on our goals and not to be discouraged by difficulties. In the workplace, we can emulate the eagle by developing a strategic vision and pursuing our goals with determination. In personal growth, the freedom and independence of the eagle encourage us to explore new opportunities and follow our unique path.

The owl, a symbol of wisdom and intuition, can guide us to make thoughtful decisions and trust our instincts. By integrating the wisdom of the owl into our daily lives, we can improve our problem-solving abilities and approach complex situations with calm and discernment.

Animal Totems for Everyone

The qualities of each animal totem can be harnessed by anyone, even by those who do not have it as their main totem. This flexible and open approach allows each of us to tap into the collective wisdom of animal totems and apply their lessons to enrich our lives.

For example, even if your main totem is not the wolf, you can still learn from its ability to cooperate and lead. If you are facing a situation that requires teamwork, you can invoke the spirit of the wolf to help you improve group dynamics and strengthen collaboration.

Similarly, you may not have the bear as your main totem, but you can still benefit from its strength and resilience. During times of stress or difficulty, you can meditate on the bear and ask for its support in finding the inner strength needed to overcome obstacles.

It is important to maintain an open and flexible mind in your approach to animal totems. Each animal has something unique to teach us, and we can draw on these lessons whenever we need them. This inclusive approach allows us to grow and evolve, continually learning from the different qualities and powers that each totem represents.

In conclusion, connecting with animal totems not only enriches our spiritual dimension but also provides practical tools to improve our daily lives. The qualities and powers of totems can be applied in various contexts, from work to personal relationships, contributing to our growth and well-being. Being flexible and open to learning from all animal totems allows us to tap into an ancient and collective wisdom, profoundly transforming our lives.

INVITATION TO DISCOVERY

In this first part of the book, we have explored the fascinating world of animal totems, understanding their meaning, importance, and the benefits of connecting with these powerful spiritual symbols. We began with a definition of animal totems, discovering how they serve as spiritual guides and protectors, and we have seen how the shamanic journey is an effective method for meeting your totem.

We have delved into the preparation techniques for the shamanic journey and provided a practical guide for conducting the journey itself. Through understanding signs and synchronicities, we have learned to recognize the attraction to a specific totem and to interpret dreams and visions that may reveal important spiritual messages to us.

A key point has been the practical application of animal totem qualities in our daily lives. We have seen how these characteristics can be used to improve various aspects of our existence, from personal relationships to professional and spiritual growth. Additionally, we have explored how the qualities of each totem can be harnessed by anyone, emphasizing the importance of flexibility and openness in approaching animal totems.

The connection with animal totems is not just a spiritual journey but a practice that can enrich our lives in profound and meaningful ways. Each totem carries with it unique wisdom that can guide and support us in times of need, offering us valuable teachings that we can apply to our daily lives.

Now that we have established a solid foundation of knowledge about animal totems, I invite you to explore and deepen your relationship with the specific totem discussed in the second part of this book. Each totem has its peculiarities and unique teachings, and dedicating time to understanding and connecting with this specific totem will allow you to gain even more personalized and powerful guidance.

The second part of the book is dedicated to a specific totem, with in-depth details on its meaning, qualities, and ways to connect with it. By exploring this section, you can discover new dimensions of your spiritual journey and find additional tools for your personal and spiritual growth.

I wish you an enlightening and transformative journey into the world of animal totems, a journey that will continue to reveal new perspectives and offer wisdom and guidance throughout your life.

THE TIGER TOTEM

Welcome to the second part of this book dedicated to animal totems, where we will explore the tiger totem in depth. If you've come this far, you probably feel a special connection with the tiger or wish to learn more about this magnificent animal and its spiritual significance. Whether you're a beginner or an experienced practitioner, this section is designed to offer you a clear, engaging guide rich with practical information to help you connect with this totem.

The tiger, often considered a symbol of strength, courage, and determination, has inspired myths and legends in many cultures. This powerful totem can offer you valuable life lessons and guide you on your spiritual journey. In the following pages, we will explore the many facets of the tiger, from its natural behavior to its shamanic significance, from the characteristics of people guided by this totem to techniques for invoking and working with the tiger's energy.

We will begin with a detailed description of the tiger, then delve into its symbolic and shamanic meanings. We will discover how to interpret dreams in which the tiger appears and what spiritual message it brings. We will also explore the associations of the tiger with numbers, stones, planets, and deities, and provide practical exercises for invoking the tiger in your daily life.

Through guided meditations, rituals, and healing practices, you will be able to experience the "medicine of the tiger" and integrate its wisdom into your life. Stories and experiences of connection with the tiger will enrich your journey, offering you inspiration and a sense of belonging to an ancient and profound tradition.

This part of the book is written to be accessible to everyone, maintaining a professional approach that respects shamanic traditions. We are confident that, with an open heart and a curious mind, you will find in these pages the tools needed for a deep and transformative connection with the tiger totem.

Prepare your spirit for a fascinating journey and let yourself be guided by the tiger through the forests of your inner self.

GENERAL DESCRIPTION

Scientific Name: Panthera tigris
Family: Felidae
Geographical Distribution: Asia (India, China, Russia, Indonesia)
Habitat: Tropical forests, temperate forests, savannas

Physical Appearance:
Length: 2.5-3.9 meters (head-body, including tail)
Shoulder Height: 90-110 cm
Weight: 100-300 kg
Fur: Orange with black stripes, white underneath

Average Age: 10-15 years in the wild, up to 20 years in captivity
Diet: Carnivore (ungulates, wild boars, buffaloes, small mammals)
Social Structure: Solitary (except during mating and raising cubs)

Communication:
Roars: Territory marking, long-distance communication
Visual and Vocal Signals: Purring, growling, tree scratching

Reproduction:
Mating Period: Variable, often year-round
Gestation Period: About 104 days
Cubs per Litter: 2-4

Endangered Species: High risk of extinction (all subspecies are threatened by habitat loss and poaching)

Danger to Humans: Moderate; attacks are rare but can be fatal, often caused by injured animals or territorial defense.

The tiger, scientifically known as *Panthera tigris*, is one of the largest and most powerful felines in the world. With its orange coat striped with black and piercing eyes, the tiger embodies strength, ferocity, and majesty. These magnificent animals are admired and respected in many cultures, often seen as symbols of power and royalty.

Physical Appearance and Behavior

Physically, tigers are enormous and powerful, with a length ranging from 2.5 to 3.9 meters, including the tail, and a shoulder height between 90 and 110 cm. Their weight can vary between 100 and 300 kg, depending on the subspecies and habitat. Tigers' fur is thick and dense, with a characteristic orange color striped with black that provides excellent camouflage in their natural environments.

Tigers are solitary predators, known for their ability to hunt stealthily and efficiently. They use their strength and agility to take down large prey such as deer, wild boars, and buffaloes. Their diet is supplemented with small mammals when necessary. They are also skilled swimmers and often cool off in rivers and lakes.

Communication and Social Structure

Tigers are solitary animals. Their communication includes powerful roars that can be heard over long distances, vocal and visual signals such as purring and tree scratching. These roars serve to mark territory and communicate with other tigers, especially during the mating season.

Tigers lead a primarily solitary life, except during mating and raising cubs. The female raises the cubs alone, teaching them hunting and protection techniques. The social structure is minimal, with interactions limited to brief periods during reproduction.

Reproduction and Longevity

The mating period of tigers can occur throughout the year. The gestation lasts about 104 days, and females give birth to 2 to 4 cubs. The cubs are born blind and completely dependent on the mother for food and protection. During the first months of life, they learn the skills needed to survive and hunt.

Tigers can live from 10 to 15 years in the wild, though in captivity they can reach 20 years. However, life in the wild is often full of dangers, including conflicts with humans, diseases, and competition with other predators.

Conservation and Interaction with Humans

Tigers are classified as an endangered species, with all subspecies threatened by habitat loss and poaching. Tiger conservation requires a concerted effort to protect their natural habitats and promote coexistence between humans and tigers.

Despite their reputation as dangerous predators, tiger attacks on humans are rare and often caused by self-defense situations or injured animals. With proper management and a better understanding of their behavior, it is possible to promote peaceful and beneficial coexistence between humans and this magnificent predator.

The tiger, with its majesty and power, represents not only a symbol of strength and courage but also a call for conservation and respect for the wild.

SHAMANIC MEANING OF THE TIGER

The tiger, powerful and majestic, is a symbol of strength and courage in the shamanic world. Considered a prominent spiritual guide, the tiger embodies the ability to act decisively and the ferocity needed to face life's challenges. Its presence in dreams and shamanic visions offers profound teachings on how to harness one's inner strength and the value of introspection.

The tiger is revered for its ability to survive in various environments, reflecting ancient wisdom and keen intelligence. This solitary animal teaches humans the importance of knowing themselves and trusting their instincts. The tiger's ability to observe and learn from its surroundings is a great lesson for those seeking to live in harmony with nature and grow spiritually. Invoking the tiger as a guide can help find the courage to face difficulties with determination and adapt to the changing circumstances of life.

An essential aspect of the tiger's symbolism is its representation of isolation and inner reflection. Tigers live and hunt alone, symbolizing the importance of spending time in solitude to reflect and regenerate. This totem reminds individuals that solitude is not a sign of weakness but an opportunity to grow and discover their inner truths. The tiger teaches us that moments of introspection are crucial for our personal and spiritual development.

In the shamanic context, the tiger is also seen as a fierce protector. Its strength and courage in defending its territory and cubs are symbols of protection and loyalty. This totem teaches us to protect what is important to us and to be faithful to our loved ones. The loyalty of the tiger is an example for building strong and lasting relationships, based on trust and mutual respect. Calling upon the tiger as a totem can provide spiritual protection and strengthen family and community bonds.

Intuition is another distinctive quality of the tiger. These animals possess a keen instinct and extraordinary sensitivity, characteristics that make them powerful totems for those seeking to develop their intuition and perceptual abilities. The tiger teaches the importance of listening to one's inner voice and trusting one's instincts, especially when it comes to making crucial decisions or overcoming difficult situations. The intuitive wisdom of the tiger can guide us towards choices that resonate deeply with our true selves.

The tiger is also an emblem of renewal and transformation. The cycles of growth and change that characterize the tiger's life reflect the natural cycles of life itself. This totem encourages us to embrace change and see transformations as opportunities for growth and rebirth. The tiger's ability to adapt and regenerate is a valuable lesson for those seeking spiritual evolution and living in harmony with nature's rhythms.

In summary, the shamanic meaning of the tiger is vast and profound, offering teachings on strength, introspection, protection, intuition, and transformation. Invoking the tiger as a totem can provide powerful and inspiring guidance, helping us live with awareness and courage, protect what we love, and follow our path with determination. The wisdom of the tiger invites us to explore our inner world and use our strength to create a life in harmony with the natural world.

CHARACTERISTICS OF THOSE WHO HAVE THIS TOTEM

People guided by the energy of the tiger possess a set of distinctive qualities that reflect the powerful and majestic nature of this totem. These individuals are often recognized for their inner strength, courage, and determination, qualities that make them natural leaders and charismatic figures in many areas of life.

One of the main characteristics of those who have the tiger as a totem is inner strength. These individuals can face challenges with extraordinary determination and resilience. They do not easily succumb to difficulties and can rise and fight even in the most adverse situations. This inner strength is not only physical but also emotional and spiritual, allowing them to navigate through life's storms with grace and power.

Courage is another distinctive quality of those influenced by the tiger. These people do not fear making bold decisions and confronting situations that might scare others. The tiger's courage manifests in the ability to act decisively and take initiatives even when circumstances are difficult or uncertain. This enables them to overcome obstacles that seem insurmountable and achieve ambitious goals.

People guided by the tiger are often very independent. Like the tiger, which is a solitary animal, these individuals value their autonomy and prefer to do things their way. They can work alone and make decisions without relying too much on others. This independence does not mean isolation but rather a confidence in themselves and their abilities that allows them to be self-sufficient and proactive.

Another important characteristic is passion. Individuals with the tiger as a totem approach life with great intensity and passion. Whether it is work, relationships, or personal interests, they put all their effort and energy into what they do. This passion makes them highly motivated and capable of inspiring others with their enthusiasm and dedication.

Sensitivity and intuition are other qualities that characterize those guided by the tiger. These individuals have a deep connection with their emotions and can perceive and understand the feelings of others with great empathy. Their intuition guides them in daily decisions, allowing them to see beyond appearances and understand the hidden dynamics of situations.

Finally, those who have the tiger as a totem possess a strong sense of protection. Just as the tiger protects its territory and cubs, these people are very protective of their loved ones and the things they care about. They are loyal and dedicated, ready to defend and support those they love in any circumstance. This quality makes them trusted friends and partners, who can always be counted on.

In summary, people guided by the tiger are strong, courageous, independent, passionate, sensitive, and protective. These qualities enable them to face life's challenges with extraordinary determination and grace, inspiring and protecting those around them. The wisdom and energy of the tiger offer powerful support for those seeking to live authentically and courageously, following their path with confidence and determination.

THE TIGER IN DREAMS

Dreaming of a tiger can be a powerful experience filled with symbolic meanings. In the shamanic context, dreams are considered a medium through which spirits and the subconscious communicate with us, offering important messages and lessons. Interpreting dreams where a tiger appears requires considering the context of the dream, the emotions felt, and specific interactions with the animal. Every detail can add nuances to the overall meaning of the dream. Below, we will explore the different interpretations of dreaming about a tiger in various situations.

Dreaming of an Aggressive Tiger

When a tiger appears in dreams with an aggressive attitude, it could symbolize an imminent challenge or a significant obstacle that you need to face in your life. The tiger, with its strength and ferocity, represents the need to draw on your inner strength and courage to overcome this difficulty. It may also indicate a part of you that is angry or frustrated and needs to be acknowledged and managed. The tiger's aggression could be an invitation to examine your repressed emotions and find constructive ways to express them.

Dreaming of Being Chased by a Tiger

Being chased by a tiger in a dream may reflect a feeling of being overwhelmed or threatened by something in your life. This could be a personal issue, a professional conflict, or a fear that you are avoiding. The tiger chasing you represents the need to face these fears and challenges directly, rather than running away from them. This type of dream may also suggest that you are ignoring an important part of your nature or emotions and that it is time to confront these aspects with courage and determination.

Dreaming of Riding a Tiger

Riding a tiger in a dream is a powerful symbol of dominance and control over your inner forces and instincts. It indicates that you have achieved a level of balance and harmony with your wild and powerful energies. This dream can suggest that you are able to face challenges with confidence and that you have the strength needed to overcome obstacles. It also represents a period of personal growth and self-discovery, where you are learning to manage and channel your energies positively.

Dreaming of a Caged Tiger

A caged tiger in your dreams can symbolize a feeling of limitation or being trapped in a situation in your life. This could relate to a job, a relationship, or a project that makes you feel constrained and unable to express your true nature. The tiger, a symbol of strength and freedom, when imprisoned, reflects your own struggle to free yourself from restrictions and find a way to express yourself fully. This dream may be a call to examine areas of your life where you feel stuck and to seek ways to regain your freedom and personal power.

Dreaming of Being a Tiger

Dreaming of being a tiger can represent a deep sense of empowerment and connection with your inner strength. This dream suggests that you are embracing the qualities of the tiger – such as strength, courage, and independence – and that you are integrating these characteristics into your daily life. It may also indicate a phase of personal transformation where you are becoming more aware of your power and your ability to act with determination. This dream is a positive sign of personal growth and the development of your self-esteem.

Dreaming of a Talking Tiger

If a tiger talks to you in a dream, the message you receive can be of great importance. Talking animals in dreams often represent the subconscious trying to communicate with you in a clear and direct way. The tiger might offer wisdom, advice, or warnings that are relevant to your current life. Pay attention to the words and tone of the tiger in the dream, as they can provide valuable insights on how to handle specific situations or which direction to take in your spiritual journey.

Dreaming of Watching a Tiger from Afar

Watching a tiger from afar in a dream can indicate a phase of reflection and observation in your life. You may be in a period where you are assessing your strengths and goals, trying to understand how to proceed. This dream suggests that you are taking time to observe and understand situations before acting, a behavior that can lead to wiser and more thoughtful decisions. The distance between you and the tiger may also reflect a desire for connection with your inner power, but with a cautious and respectful approach.

Dreaming of a tiger is an experience rich in symbolic meanings that can offer profound teachings and insights. Whether the tiger appears as an adversary, a guide, or a part of you, each dream carries a message that can help you better understand yourself and your spiritual path. Interpreting these dreams requires paying attention to the details and reflecting on the emotions and situations that accompany them. The tiger, with its strength and majesty, continues to be a powerful symbol of transformation and personal growth in the realms of the spirit and the subconscious.

SPIRITUAL MESSAGE

The tiger, as a totem animal, carries with it a profound and transformative spiritual message. Its spirit invites us to awaken our inner strength, recognize our innate courage, and live with determination and passion. The message of the tiger is a call to primal power, introspection, and the protection of our deepest truths.

"Recognize your inner strength and your ability to act with determination. Like the tiger, you possess the ferocity and passion to pursue what you desire."

Reflecting on this phrase helps us understand the deep spiritual message that the tiger, as a totem, offers us. The tiger is a symbol of power, courage, and passion, and it invites us to awaken these qualities within ourselves. In the hustle and bustle of daily life, it's easy to forget the strength that resides within us. The tiger reminds us to recognize and accept this strength, to not hide from our true power, but to embrace it with confidence and determination.

Possessing the ferocity of the tiger doesn't necessarily mean being aggressive, but rather having the courage to face life's challenges without hesitation. It means knowing when it's time to act and doing so with unwavering conviction. The tiger teaches us that true strength doesn't just lie in physicality but also in the ability to persevere, to stay focused on our goals, and to pursue them with passion.

Passion is another crucial aspect of the tiger's spiritual message. Passion drives us to give our best, to put our heart into everything we do. When we are passionate, our actions are fueled by an energy that goes beyond mere willpower; they become expressions of our deepest being. The tiger inspires us to find that spark within us, to follow our dreams and desires with all our heart.

Recognizing one's inner strength is a process of self-discovery and acceptance. It means looking within honestly, acknowledging one's abilities and potential, and having the courage to express them. This message invites us to reflect on how we can cultivate and manifest our inner strength in daily life. Perhaps it involves facing a difficult situation with courage, or making an important decision with determination.

The tiger teaches us to be leaders in our lives. Its powerful and majestic presence inspires us to take control of our destiny, to not let external circumstances overwhelm us. Just as the tiger guides its movements with precision and confidence, so too can we guide our lives with clarity and determination.

Finally, the tiger invites us to connect with our wild and instinctive nature. In a world often dominated by rationality and control, the tiger reminds us of the importance of listening to our instincts and trusting our feelings. This not only helps us make more authentic decisions but also connects us more deeply with our true essence.

In summary, the spiritual message of the tiger is an invitation to recognize and use our inner strength, to pursue our desires with passion, and to live with courage and determination. The tiger inspires us to be leaders in our lives, to connect with our instincts, and to express our true potential. Through the wisdom of the tiger, we can find the strength and guidance needed to face life's challenges and to live in harmony with our deepest self.

VARIOUS ASSOCIATIONS

The tiger, as a totem animal, is rich in symbolism and associations that enhance its influence in the spiritual world. These associations offer further levels of understanding and connection with the tiger, providing practical and symbolic tools to integrate its wisdom into daily life. Let's explore some of the main associations of the tiger, including its related number, stone, planet, and deities.

Associated Number: 4

The number 4 is closely associated with the tiger and holds deep meanings. In numerology, 4 represents stability, solid foundations, and determination. These qualities reflect the nature of the tiger, known for its strength and ability to act with precision and control. The number 4 invites the building of solid foundations in one's life, symbolizing the need to be grounded and well-structured. For those guided by the tiger, the number 4 can serve as a reminder of the importance of stability and having a solid structure on which to base one's actions and decisions.

Associated Stone: Tiger's Eye

Tiger's eye is a precious stone known for its protective and empowering properties. This stone, with its warm colors and golden streaks, reflects the majesty and power of the tiger. Tiger's eye is used to stimulate courage, strength, and self-confidence, protecting the wearer from negative energies. Like the tiger, this stone embodies the ferocity and determination needed to face life's challenges. Using tiger's eye can help channel the energy of the tiger, promoting greater focus and determination in pursuing one's goals.

Associated Planet: Mars

Mars, the red planet, is closely linked to the tiger's energy. Mars symbolizes action, determination, and passion, qualities that perfectly mirror the nature of the tiger. This planet represents vital energy and the drive to pursue what we desire with strength and courage. For those guided by the tiger, Mars can be seen as a source of inspiration and power, encouraging them to take initiative and not fear challenges. The energy of Mars can help channel the tiger's inner strength, enabling decisive and passionate action in every aspect of life.

Associated Deity: Durga (Hindu Mythology)

Durga, the warrior goddess of Hinduism, is often depicted riding a tiger. This deity is revered as a protector and as a force that destroys evil, embodying the power and ferocity of the tiger. Durga symbolizes divine feminine strength, protection, and courage, all qualities also characteristic of the tiger. Invoking Durga can help connect with the protective and combative energy of the tiger, offering strength and spiritual guidance. The connection with Durga can strengthen the ability to face difficulties with determination and to protect what is dear.

Associated Color: Orange and Black

The colors orange and black are iconic symbols of the

tiger and represent important aspects of its energy. Orange symbolizes vitality, energy, and passion, while black represents mystery, depth, and protection. These colors together create a balance of strength and grace, reflecting the nature of the tiger. Using these colors in meditation, clothing, or personal objects can help connect with the tiger's energy, fostering a sense of power and protection.

Associated Element: Fire

Fire is the element that most represents the tiger, symbolizing passion, transformation, and strength. Fire is a powerful energy that can destroy but also purify and renew. The tiger, with its fiery and determined nature, embodies these qualities, offering teachings on how to use one's energy to transform and regenerate. Connecting with the fire element can help awaken inner passion and channel the tiger's energy to face challenges and pursue goals with ardor and determination.

Associated Lunar Phase: Full Moon

The full moon is associated with the tiger due to its culminating and powerful energy. During the full moon, energies are at their peak, reflecting the intense and vigorous nature of the tiger. The full moon is a time of realization and manifestation, a moment to reap the rewards of one's work and to celebrate one's strength and successes. Meditating or performing rituals during the full moon can help connect with the tiger's energy, fostering a sense of fulfillment and personal power.

Associated Tree: Banyan

The banyan is a sacred tree in many Asian cultures, symbolizing stability, growth, and interconnection. Like the tiger, which represents strength and resilience, the banyan embodies solidity and the ability to withstand adversity. This tree, with its deep and branching roots, offers refuge and protection, similar to how the tiger protects its territory. Connecting with the banyan's energy can strengthen the sense of stability and grounding, providing a solid base from which to draw strength and courage.

These various associations offer a rich understanding of the qualities and energies associated with the tiger as a totem. Each element, from numerology to colors, from stones to planets, contributes to creating a complete picture of how to connect and work with the tiger's energy in daily life. By harnessing these connections, one can deepen their understanding and relationship with this powerful totem, integrating its wisdom and strength into their spiritual and personal journey.

HOW TO INVOKE THE TIGER IN DAILY LIFE

Invoking the tiger in daily life can be a deeply transformative and enriching experience. There are various practices and rituals that can help you connect with the tiger's energy, allowing you to integrate its wisdom and power into your life. Below, we will explore some practical techniques to invoke the tiger and harness its power in everyday life.

MEDITATIONS AND DAILY RITUALS

Building an Altar Dedicated to the Tiger

Creating an altar dedicated to the tiger is a tangible and spiritual way to honor and invoke the energy of this totem animal. This sacred space will serve as a focal point for meditation, rituals, and daily reflection, allowing you to connect more deeply with the tiger and integrate its wisdom into your life.

The first step is to choose a quiet and meaningful place in your home or outdoors where you can build your altar. This space should be easily accessible but not too exposed, maintaining a sense of sanctity and privacy. It could be a corner of your room, a shelf, a table, or a small area in your garden. Before starting to build the altar, it is essential to clean the space physically and spiritually. Remove any dust or unnecessary objects, and then purify the area using methods like smudging with sage, incense, or other purifying herbs. This helps remove negative energies and prepares the space for your sacred altar.

To start, choose a base for your altar. It could be a cloth, a tablecloth, or a small rug that covers the surface you'll be working on. Choose colors that remind you of the tiger and its energy, such as orange, black, gold, or white. This cloth serves as a base on which you will place the other elements of the altar. Place images of the tiger on the altar. These could be photographs, drawings, paintings, or statues. These images serve as visual representations of the tiger and help focus your intention during meditation and rituals. You can also include symbols associated with the tiger, such as claws, fangs, or totemic art.

Add stones and crystals that resonate with the tiger's energy. Tiger's eye is particularly powerful for this purpose, but you can also include other stones like amber, citrine quartz, or carnelian. Place these stones harmoniously on the altar, perhaps creating a small circle or a formation that inspires you. Candles are an important element for any altar. Choose candles in colors that represent the tiger and fire, such as orange, yellow, or red. Lighting a candle during your rituals can help create a sacred atmosphere and invite the tiger's energy.

Include natural elements like plants, flowers, shells, feathers, and pieces of wood. These elements help you connect with nature and bring the essence of the tiger into your sacred space. For example, you could use bamboo stalks, palm leaves, or hibiscus flowers, all associated with the tiger and its powerful qualities. Add personal objects that have special meaning for you and that you want to dedicate to the tiger's energy. These could include jewelry, amulets, stones found during walks, or other objects that evoke a sense of connection with the tiger. These personal items make the altar unique and deeply meaningful.

Once you have arranged all the elements on the altar, take a moment to officially dedicate this space to the tiger. Light a candle and say a prayer or intention, asking the tiger to bless and protect the altar. Express your gratitude for its presence and guidance in your life. Keeping the altar clean and updated is important for maintaining its energy alive and vibrant. Change the candles and offerings regularly and purify the space occasionally with incense or smudging herbs. Visit the altar daily or weekly, even for just a few minutes, to keep the connection with the tiger strong and present.

Meditation with the Tiger

Meditating with the tiger is a powerful tool for connecting deeply with the energy and wisdom of this totem animal. Find a quiet place where you won't be disturbed. Sit or lie down in a comfortable position, close your eyes, and start breathing deeply, relaxing your body and mind.

Imagine yourself in a lush jungle. Feel the soft ground beneath you and listen to the sound of leaves rustling in the wind. The fresh scent of the earth and trees envelops you, creating a sense of peace and connection with nature. As you breathe deeply, visualize a tiger appearing among the trees, slowly approaching you. Observe the details of its appearance: the color of its stripes, the intensity of its eyes, its calm and assured posture.

The tiger approaches and sits in front of you, looking

directly into your eyes. Feel its powerful and reassuring energy surrounding you. Begin communicating telepathically with the tiger, asking it to guide you on a spiritual journey. The tiger rises and starts walking, inviting you to follow. Together, you delve deeper into the jungle, exploring hidden paths and crossing sparkling streams.

As you follow the tiger, you feel your connection with it growing stronger. Listen to the messages the tiger has for you, paying attention to any images, words, or sensations that emerge. The tiger might show you aspects of yourself that you have neglected or guide you toward a greater understanding of your current challenges. Welcome these messages with gratitude and openness.

After walking for a while, the tiger leads you to a bright clearing. In the center of the clearing, there is a flat stone on which it invites you to sit. As you sit, the tiger curls up next to you, offering its protection and companionship. Feel the earth beneath you and the deep connection with nature and the tiger's spirit.

Stay in this state of meditation for a few minutes, absorbing the healing energy and wisdom of the tiger. When you feel ready, thank the tiger for its guidance and protection. Imagine slowly returning to your physical body, bringing with you the messages and insights you received.

Finally, open your eyes and take a moment to reflect on your experience. Write down your feelings and the messages received in a journal to remember them and integrate them into your daily life. Guided meditation with the tiger can become a regular practice to strengthen your bond with this powerful totem animal and to receive its guidance and protection in your spiritual journey.

Tiger's Roar

The tiger's roar is a powerful and symbolic call, loaded with spiritual and practical meanings. This practice can help you attune to the tiger's energy, release repressed emotions, and strengthen your connection with the totem animal. Here's a guide to practicing the tiger's roar.

Find a quiet and isolated place where you feel comfortable and won't be disturbed. This can be outdoors in nature or in a quiet room in your home. Make sure the space is free from distractions and that you feel safe to express yourself freely.

Start the practice by centering your mind and body. Sit or stand comfortably, close your eyes, and breathe deeply for a few minutes. Slowly inhale through your nose, filling your lungs, and then exhale gently through your mouth. Focus on your breath and allow each exhale to release tension and stress.

When you feel relaxed and centered, imagine yourself as a tiger in the jungle. Visualize the beauty of the nature around you, the freshness of the air, and the solidity of the ground beneath your feet. Feel the deep connection with the earth and with other members of the pack, even if you don't see them physically.

Now, allow the sound of the roar to emerge from deep within you. Start with a low, slow sound, similar to a gentle growl. As you become more comfortable, gradually increase the intensity and duration of the roar. Let the sound grow and expand, filling the space around you. Don't worry about how it sounds, but focus on the energy and emotion you're expressing.

As you roar, imagine calling your spiritual pack, communicating with spirit guides, and strengthening your connection with the tiger totem. Feel free to vary the tones and rhythms of the roar, allowing your body to move naturally with the sound. You might want to stretch your arms towards the sky or bend forward, following the instinct of the moment.

Continue roaring until you feel the energy has been fully expressed. It can last a few minutes or longer, depending on how you feel. When you're ready to conclude, let the roar gradually fade, returning to a deep and regular breath. Sit or stand in silence for a moment, absorbing the energy you've generated and feeling the inner peace.

Finally, open your eyes and take a moment to reflect on the experience. Notice how you feel physically, emotionally, and spiritually. If you wish, write down your feelings in a journal to track your growth and connection with the tiger. Practicing the tiger's roar can become a regular routine, helping you release emotions, tune into your intuition, and strengthen your bond with the totem animal.

Tiger Amulets and Talismans

Tiger amulets and talismans are powerful spiritual tools that can help you connect with the energy and wisdom of this totem animal. Carrying a tiger amulet or talisman with you can serve as a constant reminder of its presence, offering you protection, guidance, and inspiration in your daily life. Here's how to create and use amulets and talismans dedicated to the tiger.

To begin, it's important to choose an object that represents the tiger and resonates with you personally. This object could be a tiger-shaped pendant, a small sculpture, a stone like tiger's eye, or any other object that symbolizes the tiger for you. When choosing your amulet or talisman, trust your intuition: the tiger is known for its ability to follow its instincts, and doing the same will help you find the right object.

Once you've chosen the object, the next step is to consecrate it, meaning charging it with the energy and intent of connection with the tiger. Find a quiet place where you can focus without distractions. Hold the amulet in your hands and close your eyes. Breathe deeply and visualize the image of a tiger, imagining connecting with its spirit. You can also say a prayer or intention, asking the tiger to bless and protect the object, infusing it with its wisdom and strength. Feel free to use words that come from the heart, as personal intent is what makes the amulet powerful.

Carrying the amulet or talisman with you daily can strengthen your connection with the tiger. You can wear it as jewelry, keep it in your pocket, or place it in a meaningful location like your personal altar. Each time you touch or look at the amulet, remember the presence of the tiger and the qualities you wish to integrate into your life. This simple gesture can help you feel supported and guided in difficult situations or moments of uncertainty.

Tiger amulets and talismans can also be used during meditations or specific rituals. Before starting a meditation, hold the amulet in your hands and focus your mind on the tiger's energy. Let the amulet help you enter a state of tranquility and receptivity, facilitating a deeper connection with the totem animal. During rituals, place the amulet on the altar or keep it close to you to amplify the energy and intent of the rite.

In addition to physical objects, you can create temporary amulets using symbols and drawings. Draw a tiger on a piece of paper or carve a tiger symbol on a piece of wood. These amulets can be carried with you, placed under your pillow to influence dreams, or burned as part of a liberation or transformation ritual. Even if temporary, these amulets can have a powerful spiritual impact, helping you manifest the tiger's qualities in your life.

Finally, it's important to remember that caring for amulets and talismans is essential to maintain their effectiveness. Purify them regularly, especially after using them in particularly intense situations or when you feel they have absorbed negative energies. You can purify them with sage smoke, incense, spring water, or by leaving them under the light of the full moon. This process not only renews the energy of the amulet but also reinforces your intention of connection with the tiger.

In summary, tiger amulets and talismans are powerful tools that can offer protection, guidance, and inspiration. By creating and using these objects with intention and respect, you can strengthen your connection with the tiger and integrate its wisdom into your daily life. Whether you choose a pendant, a stone, or a drawn symbol, the important thing is the meaning and intent you attribute to the object, allowing the tiger to accompany and support you on your spiritual journey.

Creating Totem Art

Creating totem art dedicated to the tiger is a powerful and personal way to connect with this totem animal. Through art, we can express our admiration for the tiger, integrate its energy into our daily lives, and deepen our understanding of its wisdom and symbolism. Here are some ideas and suggestions for creating totem art inspired by the tiger.

To begin, it's helpful to dedicate some time to reflection and meditation on the tiger. Think about what it represents for you and which qualities you wish to manifest in your life. You might want to explore images and symbols related to the tiger, study its anatomy, or read myths and legends in which the tiger plays an important role. This preparation phase will help you gather inspiration and clarify the intent behind your artistic creation.

Once you have a clear vision of what you want to

represent, choose the artistic method that inspires you the most. You can paint, draw, sculpt, create collages, or use natural materials like wood, stones, and feathers. Each method offers a unique way to express the tiger's energy and can be chosen based on your artistic preferences and skills. If you are a painter, you might create a portrait of the tiger in a natural setting, capturing its majesty and wild spirit. If you prefer drawing, you might create a mandala or geometric design that incorporates tiger symbols, like paw prints, stylized roars, or totemic figures.

Working with natural materials can add a level of depth and connection to your totem art. You can collect stones, wood, leaves, and other elements during your walks in nature and use them to create sculptures or installations. For example, you could carve a tiger from a piece of wood found during a walk in the woods, or create a mosaic with stones and shells forming the image of a tiger. These natural materials not only add texture and visual interest to your work but also carry the energy and spirit of the places they come from.

Another idea is to create an art journal dedicated to the tiger. This can be a notebook in which you draw, paint, and write reflections on the tiger and your connection with it. You can include sketches, quotes, poems, and photographs that evoke the essence of the tiger. This journal can become a personal and precious collection of experiences, insights, and inspirations related to the tiger, which you can consult and enrich over time.

Music and dance are other forms of totem art that can be used to connect with the tiger. You can compose a melody or song inspired by the tiger, using instruments that evoke nature and the sounds of the jungle. If you prefer dance, you can create choreography that mimics the fluid and graceful movements of the tiger, using dance as a ritual to invoke its energy. These forms of performing art can be particularly powerful for releasing emotions and creating a state of trance or deep meditation.

In summary, creating totem art dedicated to the tiger is a deep and personal way to honor this totem animal and integrate its energy into your life. Whether you choose to paint, sculpt, draw, dance, or create objects with natural materials, let your heart and intuition guide you. Through art, you can explore and manifest the tiger's wisdom, creating works that not only beautify your space but also enrich your spiritual journey.

THE MEDICINE OF THE TIGER

The medicine of the tiger represents a set of practices and teachings that this totemic animal offers for our physical, emotional, and spiritual well-being. In shamanic tradition, "medicine" refers to the healing power and spiritual lessons that a totem animal can bring into our lives. The tiger, with its strength, courage, and determination, offers us various practices that we can use to heal and strengthen ourselves. Here are some of the most powerful healing practices associated with the medicine of the tiger.

Healing Practices with the Tiger

The tiger is known for its healing qualities and protective power. Invoking the medicine of the tiger can support your physical and spiritual well-being in many ways. One of the most common and accessible practices is using visualization to imagine the tiger healing you. Find a quiet place where you won't be disturbed, lie down comfortably, and close your eyes. Breathe deeply to relax and center yourself.

Visualize a tiger appearing before you, majestic and serene. Imagine this tiger approaching you and beginning to surround you with its healing energy. Feel this energy as warmth or light spreading through your body. With each breath, imagine the tiger removing any negativity or blockages from your body and mind, filling you with strength, vitality, and serenity. This practice can be particularly useful during times of illness or stress, helping you recover faster and maintain emotional balance.

During the visualization, you can also ask the tiger to show you images or messages that help you better understand the causes of your discomfort and find solutions to improve your health. Take as much time as you need for this meditation, and when you feel ready, thank the tiger for its assistance and slowly open your eyes. Repeat this practice regularly to maintain a constant connection with the medicine of the tiger.

Tiger Dance

Dance is a powerful way to channel the tiger's energy and release repressed emotions. The tiger dance can help you release physical and mental tensions, allowing you to deeply connect with your instinct and wild nature. To start, create a safe space where you can move freely. This space can be a quiet room in your home, a corner of your garden, or any place where you feel comfortable.

Play rhythmic music that inspires you and makes you feel connected to nature. Start moving slowly, allowing your body to warm up and relax. Mimic the fluid and graceful movements of a tiger. You can think of tigers moving stealthily through the jungle, hunting with precision, resting, or playing with each other. Let your body freely express these images and sensations.

Don't worry about how you look or if your movements aren't perfect. The goal is to let go of control and allow your body to move spontaneously. The tiger dance will help you release blocked energies and connect with your inner strength. It can also be an opportunity to explore and accept parts of yourself that you may have neglected or repressed.

As you dance, imagine yourself transforming into a tiger. Feel strong, agile, and free. Let this transformation bring you a new awareness of your body and emotions. You can also use the tiger dance as a healing ritual, focusing on a specific intention, such as releasing stress, healing an emotional wound, or inviting new positive energies into your life.

After dancing, take a moment to sit in silence and reflect on the experience. Notice how you feel physically, emotionally, and spiritually. Write down your feelings and insights in a journal to track your growth and healing journey with the medicine of the tiger. The tiger dance can become a regular practice that helps you stay connected with the totem animal and maintain balance in your life.

Invoking the medicine of the tiger through these healing practices can bring deep benefits and transformations. Whether you choose to use visualization, dance, or both, the important thing is to perform these practices with intention and openness. Let the wisdom and strength of the tiger guide you on your journey of well-being and spiritual growth.

MYTHOLOGY AND FOLKLORE

The tiger is one of the most fascinating and revered animals in many cultures around the world. Its majesty, strength, and ferocity have made it a powerful and respected symbol, often associated with deities, legends, and myths that exalt its qualities. Exploring the mythology and folklore of the tiger allows us to better understand its symbolic and spiritual significance.

Hindu Mythology

In Hindu mythology, the tiger is closely associated with the goddess Durga, one of the most venerated and powerful deities. Durga, often depicted riding a tiger, is the goddess of war and protection, symbolizing strength, courage, and determination. The tiger represents her vehemence and her power to destroy evil and protect the devotees. Legends tell that Durga defeated the demon Mahishasura, who had terrorized gods and humans, using the tiger's strength and agility to overpower him. This image of Durga on the tiger is a symbol of divine power and protection, inspiring devotees to find strength and courage in their daily battles.

Chinese Mythology

In China, the tiger is one of the Four Celestial Animals and represents the west, autumn, and metal in ancient Chinese cosmology. Known as the White Tiger, it is seen as a powerful guardian and a symbol of strength and courage. The White Tiger is also associated with protection against evil spirits and negative influences. During Chinese New Year, it is common to see depictions of tigers used as protective talismans to ward off bad luck and bring good fortune. The tiger is also a zodiac sign in the Chinese calendar, and people born under this sign are considered brave, confident, and passionate.

Korean Folklore

In Korea, the tiger is a national symbol and a central element in Korean folklore. Often regarded as a protector of nature and people, the tiger appears in many legends as a wise and benevolent creature. A famous legend tells of a tiger that befriended a young boy and helped him overcome various difficulties, becoming a sort of spiritual guide for him. This story illustrates the role of the tiger as a protector and a symbol of wisdom and friendship.

Japanese Mythology

In Japan, the tiger is seen as a symbol of strength, courage, and protection. Ancient Japanese legends tell of tigers that guard temples and homes from demons and negative energies. Tigers are also associated with samurai warriors, who admired their strength and agility. The tiger is considered a model of courage and discipline, essential qualities for samurai. Additionally, Japanese art often depicts tigers in dynamic and powerful poses, highlighting their grace and ferocity.

Southeast Asian Legends

In Southeast Asia, the tiger is revered as a sacred and powerful animal. Indigenous tribes in this region tell stories of tiger spirits that protect forests and communities. Shamans often invoke the tiger spirit during healing and protection rituals. In many of these cultures, it is believed that ancestors can reincarnate as tigers to watch over their descendants. The tiger is also a symbol of fertility and prosperity, and many rites of passage and auspicious ceremonies involve offerings and prayers directed at the tiger.

The Tiger in European Legends

Although the tiger is not native to Europe, it appears in many European legends and popular stories due to the influence of explorations and colonies. Tigers were often seen as exotic and dangerous creatures, symbols of the wild and the unknown. In medieval bestiaries, the tiger was described as a fierce and invincible animal, capable of instilling fear and respect. These descriptions reflect the admiration and fear that tigers inspired in European peoples.

Symbolism and Interpretation

In all these traditions, the tiger represents a range of powerful and inspiring qualities: strength, courage, protection, wisdom, and independence. These stories and legends not only exalt the physical characteristics of the tiger but also highlight its spiritual and symbolic significance. The tiger, as a totemic animal, invites us to find our inner strength, protect ourselves from negativity, and follow our path with courage and determination.

The mythology and folklore of the tiger offer us a deep

insight into the role of this animal in the spiritual and cultural world. These stories inspire us to connect with the tiger's energy and integrate its qualities into our daily lives. Whether you are seeking protection, strength, or wisdom, the tiger can be a powerful guide and a symbol of personal transformation.

TEACHINGS AND LIFE LESSONS

The tiger, as a totemic animal, offers a wide range of teachings and life lessons that can inspire and guide us on our spiritual and everyday journey. These teachings stem from the tiger's innate characteristics and its cultural and spiritual symbolism. Exploring these teachings allows us to better understand how to integrate the tiger's wisdom into our lives.

One of the main teachings of the tiger is the importance of strength and courage. The tiger is a powerful and determined predator, capable of facing challenges with enviable resolve. This animal teaches us to find our inner strength and use it to overcome the obstacles we encounter along our path. The tiger reminds us that, regardless of difficulties, we have within us the ability to face and overcome any situation with courage and determination. Learning to channel this strength can help us become more resilient and confident.

The tiger is also an expert hunter, knowing when it is time to act and when it is time to wait. This teaching is fundamental in our daily lives, where we are often tempted to act impulsively or rush things. The tiger teaches us the importance of patience and precision. Waiting for the right moment to act can make the difference between success and failure. Learning to be patient and plan carefully allows us to achieve better results and avoid mistakes that could cost us dearly.

The tiger walks with grace and confidence, aware of its strength and abilities. This teaches us the importance of self-confidence and believing in our skills. Often, a lack of confidence can prevent us from reaching our goals or seizing the opportunities life offers us. The tiger reminds us that we must believe in ourselves and our ability to face challenges. Cultivating self-confidence not only helps us overcome difficulties but also allows us to live a fuller and more satisfying life.

Tigers are solitary animals, living and hunting on their own. This aspect of their nature teaches us the importance of independence and autonomy. Learning to rely on ourselves and make independent decisions is crucial for our personal and spiritual growth. The tiger encourages us to develop our skills and trust our instincts. Being independent does not mean being isolated, but rather being able to support ourselves and make choices that reflect our values and desires.

Although the tiger is a symbol of strength and power, it is also an animal that can show kindness and care, especially towards its cubs. This teaching reminds us of the importance of finding a balance between strength and kindness in our lives. Being strong does not mean being aggressive or insensitive. True strength includes the ability to be kind, empathetic, and show compassion towards others. The tiger teaches us that we can be powerful and at the same time loving and caring.

The tiger is deeply connected to its natural environment, living in harmony with the jungle and its resources. This teaches us the importance of connecting with nature and respecting our environment. Spending time in nature, observing animals and plants, and appreciating the beauty of the natural world can have a profoundly rejuvenating effect on our mind and spirit. The tiger invites us to reconnect with nature and live in a more sustainable and respectful way towards the planet.

With its innate courage, the tiger teaches us to face our fears. Instead of avoiding or repressing them, we must acknowledge them and find the strength to overcome them. This process can be difficult and requires time, but it is essential for our personal and spiritual growth. The tiger shows us that facing fears can lead to greater self-awareness and a more free and fulfilling life.

The teachings of the tiger are numerous and profound, offering valuable lessons that we can apply to our daily lives. Whether it's finding our inner strength, cultivating patience, developing self-confidence, or connecting with nature, the tiger guides us towards a more balanced, courageous, and authentic life. By integrating these teachings into our existence, we can grow spiritually and live with greater awareness and harmony. The tiger, with its majesty and wisdom, inspires us to be the best version of ourselves, to live courageously, and to follow our path with determination.

Thank you for taking the time and attention to read this book. It has been a fascinating journey through the world of animal totems, with a particular focus on the Tiger and the profound spiritual connections this majestic animal carries. I hope you have found inspiration, knowledge, and useful tools for your personal and spiritual journey.

I would like to invite you to leave a review on Amazon. Your opinion is valuable, and your reviews help other readers discover and appreciate this work. Whether you found the book enlightening, whether it sparked new questions, or offered new perspectives, sharing your experience can make a difference. A positive and sincere review not only supports the author but also enriches the community of readers and enthusiasts of spirituality and animal totems.

Thank you again for your support, and may you continue on your journey of discovery and personal growth. May the tiger and all animal totems guide and protect you always.

With gratitude,
Valerio

OTHER BOOKS BY THE AUTHOR

-Sciamanesimo Runico, Valerio Barsacchi, 2023

-Arcangeli e Maestri Ascesi, Valerio Barsacchi, 2023

-Animali Totem: Segreti, Simbolismi e connessioni Spirituali, Valerio Barsacchi, 2023

-Cristalloterapia: L'arte di guarire con le pietre, Valerio Barsacchi, 2023

-Mandala degli Animali Totem, Valerio Barsacchi, 2023

-Mandala degli Arcani Maggiori, Valerio Barsacchi, 2023

-Sciamanesimo Facile, Valerio Barsacchi, 2023

-Dizionario Sciamanico dei Nomi, Valerio Barsacchi, 2024

-Miti Da Colorare: arteterapia e meditazione con le divinità nordiche, Valerio Barsacchi, 2024

-Miti Da Colorare: arteterapia e meditazione con le divinità greche, Valerio Barsacchi, 2024

-Numerologia Sciamanica: Scopri i tuoi archetipi e trasforma la tua vita, Valerio Barsacchi, 2024

Use this space to note down your reflections and thoughts

Use this space to note down your reflections and thoughts

Use this space to note down your reflections and thoughts

AUTHOR'S NOTE

The information contained in this book regarding animal totems, including their meanings and associated practices, comes from various cultural and spiritual traditions. It is important to remember that totems can be interpreted in different and unique ways from tradition to tradition and even from person to person. The descriptions and teachings presented in these pages are not intended to be absolute truths, but rather guidelines that can enrich one's personal journey.

Each individual may have a different experience with animal totems and may find unique and deeply personal meanings in their symbolism.

Printed in Great Britain
by Amazon

59089584R00047